50 Summer Salad Recipes

By: Kelly Johnson

Table of Contents

- Caprese Salad with Fresh Mozzarella
- Watermelon Feta Salad with Mint
- Grilled Peach and Arugula Salad
- Cucumber Tomato Salad with Red Onion
- Quinoa Salad with Black Beans and Corn
- Greek Salad with Olives and Feta
- Spinach Strawberry Salad with Poppy Seed Dressing
- Avocado and Grapefruit Salad
- Chickpea Salad with Parsley and Lemon
- Asian Noodle Salad with Sesame Dressing
- Panzanella (Italian Bread Salad)
- Summer Pasta Salad with Vegetables
- Berry Salad with Goat Cheese
- Mediterranean Couscous Salad
- Classic Coleslaw with Cabbage and Carrots
- Mixed Green Salad with Balsamic Vinaigrette
- Tomato and Mozzarella Salad with Basil
- Shrimp and Avocado Salad
- Zucchini Noodle Salad with Cherry Tomatoes
- Grilled Corn Salad with Lime Dressing
- Fattoush Salad with Pita Chips
- Roasted Beet Salad with Walnuts
- Cilantro Lime Rice Salad
- Thai Beef Salad with Peanuts
- Roasted Vegetable Salad with Quinoa
- Citrus Salad with Mixed Greens
- Pesto Pasta Salad with Sun-Dried Tomatoes
- Cabbage and Apple Salad with Pecans
- Thai Mango Salad with Lime Dressing
- Couscous Salad with Chickpeas and Veggies
- Grilled Chicken Salad with Avocado
- Roasted Cauliflower Salad with Tahini
- Mixed Bean Salad with Italian Dressing
- Strawberry Spinach Salad with Almonds
- Grilled Chicken Caesar Salad
- Rainbow Salad with Bell Peppers and Carrots

- Egg and Potato Salad with Mustard Dressing
- Lobster Salad with Lemon and Dill
- Green Bean Salad with Cherry Tomatoes
- Asian Cabbage Salad with Sesame Dressing
- Mediterranean Chickpea Salad
- Antipasto Salad with Salami and Cheese
- Smoked Salmon Salad with Capers
- Kale Salad with Cranberries and Pecans
- Avocado and Black Bean Salad
- Roasted Tomato Salad with Fresh Basil
- Chicken and Avocado Salad
- Summer Fruit Salad with Honey Lime Dressing
- Tomato and Cucumber Salad with Dill
- Greek Orzo Salad with Lemon Dressing

Caprese Salad with Fresh Mozzarella

Ingredients:

- 4 ripe tomatoes, sliced
- 8 oz fresh mozzarella, sliced
- Fresh basil leaves
- 2 tablespoons balsamic glaze
- 2 tablespoons extra virgin olive oil
- Salt and pepper to taste

Instructions:

1. **Layer Ingredients:** On a serving platter, alternate layers of sliced tomatoes and mozzarella.
2. **Add Basil:** Tuck fresh basil leaves between the layers.
3. **Drizzle:** Drizzle with balsamic glaze and olive oil.
4. **Season and Serve:** Sprinkle with salt and pepper. Serve immediately.

Watermelon Feta Salad with Mint

Ingredients:

- 4 cups watermelon, cubed
- 1 cup feta cheese, crumbled
- 1/4 cup fresh mint leaves, chopped
- Juice of 1 lime
- Salt and pepper to taste

Instructions:

1. **Combine Ingredients:** In a large bowl, combine watermelon, feta cheese, and mint.
2. **Add Lime Juice:** Drizzle with lime juice and season with salt and pepper.
3. **Toss and Serve:** Gently toss the salad and serve chilled.

Grilled Peach and Arugula Salad

Ingredients:

- 2 ripe peaches, halved and pitted
- 4 cups arugula
- 1/2 cup goat cheese, crumbled
- 1/4 cup walnuts, toasted
- 2 tablespoons olive oil
- 1 tablespoon balsamic vinegar
- Salt and pepper to taste

Instructions:

1. **Grill Peaches:** Preheat grill to medium heat. Grill peach halves for about 3-4 minutes until grill marks appear.
2. **Combine Salad:** In a large bowl, combine arugula, grilled peaches, goat cheese, and walnuts.
3. **Dress and Toss:** In a small bowl, whisk together olive oil, balsamic vinegar, salt, and pepper. Drizzle over the salad and toss gently.
4. **Serve:** Serve immediately.

Cucumber Tomato Salad with Red Onion

Ingredients:

- 2 cucumbers, diced
- 2 cups cherry tomatoes, halved
- 1/2 red onion, thinly sliced
- 2 tablespoons olive oil
- 1 tablespoon red wine vinegar
- Salt and pepper to taste
- Fresh parsley for garnish

Instructions:

1. **Combine Vegetables:** In a large bowl, combine cucumbers, tomatoes, and red onion.
2. **Dress the Salad:** In a small bowl, whisk together olive oil, vinegar, salt, and pepper. Pour over the salad.
3. **Toss and Garnish:** Toss gently and garnish with fresh parsley before serving.

Quinoa Salad with Black Beans and Corn

Ingredients:

- 1 cup quinoa, rinsed and drained
- 2 cups water
- 1 can (15 oz) black beans, rinsed and drained
- 1 cup corn (fresh or canned)
- 1 bell pepper, diced
- 1/4 cup red onion, diced
- 1/4 cup cilantro, chopped
- Juice of 1 lime
- 2 tablespoons olive oil
- Salt and pepper to taste

Instructions:

1. **Cook Quinoa:** In a saucepan, bring water to a boil. Add quinoa, reduce heat, and simmer for about 15 minutes until quinoa is fluffy. Let cool.
2. **Combine Ingredients:** In a large bowl, combine cooked quinoa, black beans, corn, bell pepper, red onion, and cilantro.
3. **Dress the Salad:** In a small bowl, whisk together lime juice, olive oil, salt, and pepper. Pour over the salad and toss gently.
4. **Serve:** Serve chilled or at room temperature.

Greek Salad with Olives and Feta

Ingredients:

- 4 cups mixed greens
- 1 cucumber, diced
- 2 cups cherry tomatoes, halved
- 1/2 red onion, sliced
- 1/2 cup Kalamata olives, pitted
- 1 cup feta cheese, crumbled
- 2 tablespoons olive oil
- 1 tablespoon red wine vinegar
- Salt and pepper to taste

Instructions:

1. **Combine Ingredients:** In a large bowl, combine mixed greens, cucumber, tomatoes, red onion, olives, and feta cheese.
2. **Dress the Salad:** In a small bowl, whisk together olive oil, vinegar, salt, and pepper. Drizzle over the salad.
3. **Toss and Serve:** Toss gently and serve immediately.

Spinach Strawberry Salad with Poppy Seed Dressing

Ingredients:

- 4 cups fresh spinach
- 2 cups strawberries, sliced
- 1/4 cup red onion, thinly sliced
- 1/4 cup pecans, toasted
- 1/4 cup feta cheese, crumbled
- 1/4 cup poppy seed dressing

Instructions:

1. **Combine Salad Ingredients:** In a large bowl, combine spinach, strawberries, red onion, pecans, and feta cheese.
2. **Add Dressing:** Drizzle with poppy seed dressing.
3. **Toss and Serve:** Toss gently to combine and serve immediately.

Avocado and Grapefruit Salad

Ingredients:

- 2 ripe avocados, sliced
- 2 grapefruits, segmented
- 1/4 red onion, thinly sliced
- 2 tablespoons olive oil
- 1 tablespoon lime juice
- Salt and pepper to taste
- Fresh cilantro for garnish

Instructions:

1. **Combine Ingredients:** In a large bowl, combine avocado slices, grapefruit segments, and red onion.
2. **Dress the Salad:** In a small bowl, whisk together olive oil, lime juice, salt, and pepper. Drizzle over the salad.
3. **Toss and Garnish:** Toss gently and garnish with fresh cilantro before serving.

Chickpea Salad with Parsley and Lemon

Ingredients:

- 1 can (15 oz) chickpeas, rinsed and drained
- 1 cup fresh parsley, chopped
- 1/2 red onion, diced
- 1/2 cucumber, diced
- Juice of 1 lemon
- 2 tablespoons olive oil
- Salt and pepper to taste

Instructions:

1. **Combine Ingredients:** In a large bowl, mix chickpeas, parsley, red onion, and cucumber.
2. **Dress the Salad:** In a small bowl, whisk together lemon juice, olive oil, salt, and pepper. Pour over the salad.
3. **Toss and Serve:** Toss gently and serve chilled or at room temperature.

Asian Noodle Salad with Sesame Dressing

Ingredients:

- 8 oz rice noodles or soba noodles
- 1 cup carrots, julienned
- 1 cup bell pepper, sliced
- 1 cup cucumber, sliced
- 1/4 cup green onions, sliced
- 1/4 cup sesame seeds

For the Dressing:

- 3 tablespoons soy sauce
- 2 tablespoons rice vinegar
- 2 tablespoons sesame oil
- 1 tablespoon honey or agave syrup
- 1 clove garlic, minced
- 1 teaspoon grated ginger

Instructions:

1. **Cook Noodles:** Cook the noodles according to package instructions, then rinse under cold water and drain.
2. **Prepare Dressing:** In a bowl, whisk together soy sauce, rice vinegar, sesame oil, honey, garlic, and ginger.
3. **Combine Ingredients:** In a large bowl, combine the noodles, carrots, bell pepper, cucumber, and green onions. Drizzle with dressing and toss to combine.
4. **Garnish:** Sprinkle sesame seeds on top before serving.

Panzanella (Italian Bread Salad)

Ingredients:

- 4 cups stale bread, cubed
- 2 cups ripe tomatoes, chopped
- 1 cucumber, diced
- 1/2 red onion, sliced
- 1/4 cup fresh basil, torn
- 1/4 cup olive oil
- 2 tablespoons red wine vinegar
- Salt and pepper to taste

Instructions:

1. **Toast Bread:** Preheat the oven to 375°F (190°C). Spread bread cubes on a baking sheet and toast for about 10-15 minutes until golden brown.
2. **Combine Ingredients:** In a large bowl, combine toasted bread, tomatoes, cucumber, red onion, and basil.
3. **Dress the Salad:** In a small bowl, whisk together olive oil, vinegar, salt, and pepper. Drizzle over the salad and toss gently.
4. **Serve:** Let the salad sit for about 15 minutes before serving to allow flavors to meld.

Summer Pasta Salad with Vegetables

Ingredients:

- 8 oz pasta (such as fusilli or penne)
- 1 cup cherry tomatoes, halved
- 1 cup bell pepper, diced
- 1 cup cucumber, diced
- 1/4 cup red onion, diced
- 1/4 cup fresh basil, chopped
- 1/4 cup Italian dressing

Instructions:

1. **Cook Pasta:** Cook pasta according to package instructions. Drain and rinse under cold water.
2. **Combine Ingredients:** In a large bowl, combine cooked pasta, cherry tomatoes, bell pepper, cucumber, red onion, and basil.
3. **Dress the Salad:** Add Italian dressing and toss to combine.
4. **Serve:** Serve chilled or at room temperature.

Berry Salad with Goat Cheese

Ingredients:

- 4 cups mixed greens
- 1 cup strawberries, sliced
- 1 cup blueberries
- 1/2 cup goat cheese, crumbled
- 1/4 cup walnuts or pecans, toasted
- 2 tablespoons balsamic vinaigrette

Instructions:

1. **Combine Ingredients:** In a large bowl, combine mixed greens, strawberries, blueberries, goat cheese, and nuts.
2. **Dress the Salad:** Drizzle with balsamic vinaigrette and toss gently.
3. **Serve:** Serve immediately.

Mediterranean Couscous Salad

Ingredients:

- 1 cup couscous
- 1 1/4 cups vegetable broth or water
- 1 cup cherry tomatoes, halved
- 1/2 cucumber, diced
- 1/4 cup Kalamata olives, pitted and sliced
- 1/4 cup red onion, diced
- 1/4 cup feta cheese, crumbled
- 2 tablespoons olive oil
- 1 tablespoon lemon juice
- Salt and pepper to taste

Instructions:

1. **Cook Couscous:** In a saucepan, bring broth or water to a boil. Stir in couscous, cover, and remove from heat. Let sit for 5 minutes, then fluff with a fork.
2. **Combine Ingredients:** In a large bowl, combine couscous, cherry tomatoes, cucumber, olives, red onion, and feta cheese.
3. **Dress the Salad:** In a small bowl, whisk together olive oil, lemon juice, salt, and pepper. Drizzle over the salad and toss to combine.
4. **Serve:** Serve chilled or at room temperature.

Classic Coleslaw with Cabbage and Carrots

Ingredients:

- 4 cups green cabbage, shredded
- 1 cup carrots, grated
- 1/2 cup mayonnaise
- 2 tablespoons apple cider vinegar
- 1 tablespoon sugar
- Salt and pepper to taste

Instructions:

1. **Combine Vegetables:** In a large bowl, combine cabbage and carrots.
2. **Make Dressing:** In a small bowl, whisk together mayonnaise, vinegar, sugar, salt, and pepper.
3. **Dress the Slaw:** Pour dressing over cabbage mixture and toss to combine.
4. **Chill and Serve:** Refrigerate for at least 30 minutes before serving to allow flavors to meld.

Mixed Green Salad with Balsamic Vinaigrette

Ingredients:

- 4 cups mixed greens
- 1/2 cup cherry tomatoes, halved
- 1/2 cucumber, sliced
- 1/4 cup red onion, thinly sliced
- 1/4 cup feta cheese, crumbled (optional)

For the Balsamic Vinaigrette:

- 1/4 cup balsamic vinegar
- 1/2 cup olive oil
- 1 teaspoon Dijon mustard
- Salt and pepper to taste

Instructions:

1. **Make Dressing:** In a small bowl, whisk together balsamic vinegar, olive oil, Dijon mustard, salt, and pepper.
2. **Combine Salad Ingredients:** In a large bowl, combine mixed greens, cherry tomatoes, cucumber, red onion, and feta cheese.
3. **Dress the Salad:** Drizzle with vinaigrette and toss to combine.
4. **Serve:** Serve immediately.

Tomato and Mozzarella Salad with Basil

Ingredients:

- 4 large tomatoes, sliced
- 8 oz fresh mozzarella, sliced
- 1/4 cup fresh basil leaves
- 2 tablespoons olive oil
- 1 tablespoon balsamic vinegar
- Salt and pepper to taste

Instructions:

1. **Arrange Ingredients:** On a serving platter, alternate slices of tomato and mozzarella. Tuck basil leaves between the layers.
2. **Dress the Salad:** Drizzle with olive oil and balsamic vinegar. Season with salt and pepper.
3. **Serve:** Serve immediately or let it sit for 15 minutes to allow flavors to meld.

Shrimp and Avocado Salad

Ingredients:

- 1 lb cooked shrimp, peeled and deveined
- 1 avocado, diced
- 1 cup cherry tomatoes, halved
- 1/4 red onion, thinly sliced
- 2 tablespoons lime juice
- 2 tablespoons olive oil
- Salt and pepper to taste
- Fresh cilantro for garnish (optional)

Instructions:

1. **Combine Ingredients:** In a large bowl, combine shrimp, avocado, cherry tomatoes, and red onion.
2. **Make Dressing:** In a small bowl, whisk together lime juice, olive oil, salt, and pepper.
3. **Dress the Salad:** Drizzle the dressing over the salad and toss gently.
4. **Garnish and Serve:** Garnish with fresh cilantro if desired and serve immediately.

Zucchini Noodle Salad with Cherry Tomatoes

Ingredients:

- 2 medium zucchinis, spiralized into noodles
- 1 cup cherry tomatoes, halved
- 1/4 cup fresh basil, chopped
- 2 tablespoons olive oil
- 1 tablespoon lemon juice
- Salt and pepper to taste

Instructions:

1. **Prepare Zoodles:** Place spiralized zucchini noodles in a large bowl.
2. **Add Other Ingredients:** Add cherry tomatoes, basil, olive oil, lemon juice, salt, and pepper.
3. **Toss and Serve:** Toss gently to combine and serve immediately.

Grilled Corn Salad with Lime Dressing

Ingredients:

- 4 ears of corn, husked and grilled
- 1 cup cherry tomatoes, halved
- 1/4 red onion, diced
- 1/4 cup fresh cilantro, chopped
- 2 tablespoons lime juice
- 2 tablespoons olive oil
- Salt and pepper to taste

Instructions:

1. **Grill Corn:** Grill corn until charred, then let cool. Cut kernels off the cob.
2. **Combine Ingredients:** In a large bowl, combine corn, cherry tomatoes, red onion, and cilantro.
3. **Make Dressing:** In a small bowl, whisk together lime juice, olive oil, salt, and pepper.
4. **Dress the Salad:** Drizzle the dressing over the salad and toss to combine. Serve chilled or at room temperature.

Fattoush Salad with Pita Chips

Ingredients:

- 2 cups mixed greens
- 1 cup cucumbers, diced
- 1 cup tomatoes, diced
- 1/4 red onion, sliced
- 1/4 cup fresh parsley, chopped
- 1/4 cup fresh mint, chopped
- 2 pita breads, toasted and broken into chips

For the Dressing:

- 1/4 cup olive oil
- 2 tablespoons lemon juice
- 1 tablespoon pomegranate molasses
- Salt and pepper to taste

Instructions:

1. **Prepare Pita Chips:** Toast pita breads until golden and crispy. Break into chips.
2. **Combine Salad Ingredients:** In a large bowl, combine mixed greens, cucumbers, tomatoes, red onion, parsley, and mint.
3. **Make Dressing:** In a small bowl, whisk together olive oil, lemon juice, pomegranate molasses, salt, and pepper.
4. **Dress the Salad:** Drizzle dressing over salad and toss gently. Top with pita chips before serving.

Roasted Beet Salad with Walnuts

Ingredients:

- 4 medium beets, roasted and sliced
- 4 cups mixed greens
- 1/2 cup walnuts, toasted
- 1/4 cup goat cheese or feta, crumbled
- 2 tablespoons balsamic vinegar
- 2 tablespoons olive oil
- Salt and pepper to taste

Instructions:

1. **Roast Beets:** Preheat oven to 400°F (200°C). Wrap beets in foil and roast for 45-60 minutes until tender. Let cool, peel, and slice.
2. **Combine Salad Ingredients:** In a large bowl, combine mixed greens, roasted beets, walnuts, and cheese.
3. **Make Dressing:** In a small bowl, whisk together balsamic vinegar, olive oil, salt, and pepper.
4. **Dress the Salad:** Drizzle dressing over the salad and toss gently. Serve immediately.

Cilantro Lime Rice Salad

Ingredients:

- 2 cups cooked rice (white or brown)
- 1 cup black beans, rinsed and drained
- 1 cup corn, cooked
- 1/2 red bell pepper, diced
- 1/4 cup red onion, diced
- 1/4 cup fresh cilantro, chopped
- Juice of 2 limes
- 2 tablespoons olive oil
- Salt and pepper to taste

Instructions:

1. **Combine Ingredients:** In a large bowl, mix cooked rice, black beans, corn, bell pepper, red onion, and cilantro.
2. **Make Dressing:** In a small bowl, whisk together lime juice, olive oil, salt, and pepper.
3. **Dress the Salad:** Pour dressing over the salad and toss to combine. Serve chilled or at room temperature.

Thai Beef Salad with Peanuts

Ingredients:

- 8 oz flank steak, grilled and sliced
- 4 cups mixed greens
- 1 cup cucumber, sliced
- 1 cup cherry tomatoes, halved
- 1/4 red onion, sliced
- 1/4 cup roasted peanuts, chopped
- 2 tablespoons fresh cilantro, chopped

For the Dressing:

- 3 tablespoons lime juice
- 2 tablespoons fish sauce
- 1 tablespoon sugar
- 1 clove garlic, minced

Instructions:

1. **Grill Steak:** Grill flank steak to desired doneness, then let rest and slice thinly.
2. **Combine Salad Ingredients:** In a large bowl, combine mixed greens, cucumber, cherry tomatoes, red onion, and cilantro.
3. **Make Dressing:** In a small bowl, whisk together lime juice, fish sauce, sugar, and garlic.
4. **Dress the Salad:** Add steak to the salad and drizzle with dressing. Top with chopped peanuts and serve immediately.

Roasted Vegetable Salad with Quinoa

Ingredients:

- 2 cups mixed vegetables (such as bell peppers, zucchini, and carrots), roasted
- 1 cup cooked quinoa
- 1/4 cup feta cheese, crumbled (optional)
- 1/4 cup fresh parsley, chopped
- 2 tablespoons olive oil
- 1 tablespoon balsamic vinegar
- Salt and pepper to taste

Instructions:

1. **Roast Vegetables:** Preheat oven to 425°F (220°C). Toss vegetables with olive oil, salt, and pepper. Roast for 20-25 minutes until tender.
2. **Combine Ingredients:** In a large bowl, mix roasted vegetables, quinoa, feta cheese, and parsley.
3. **Make Dressing:** In a small bowl, whisk together olive oil, balsamic vinegar, salt, and pepper.
4. **Dress the Salad:** Drizzle dressing over the salad and toss gently. Serve warm or at room temperature.

Citrus Salad with Mixed Greens

Ingredients:

- 4 cups mixed greens (arugula, spinach, or romaine)
- 2 oranges, peeled and segmented
- 1 grapefruit, peeled and segmented
- 1/4 red onion, thinly sliced
- 1/4 cup feta cheese, crumbled
- 1/4 cup walnuts or pecans, toasted

For the Dressing:

- 3 tablespoons olive oil
- 2 tablespoons orange juice
- 1 tablespoon honey
- Salt and pepper to taste

Instructions:

1. **Combine Salad Ingredients:** In a large bowl, toss mixed greens, citrus segments, red onion, feta cheese, and nuts.
2. **Make Dressing:** In a small bowl, whisk together olive oil, orange juice, honey, salt, and pepper.
3. **Dress the Salad:** Drizzle dressing over the salad just before serving and toss gently.

Pesto Pasta Salad with Sun-Dried Tomatoes

Ingredients:

- 8 oz pasta (fusilli or penne)
- 1/2 cup pesto (store-bought or homemade)
- 1/2 cup sun-dried tomatoes, chopped
- 1/2 cup cherry tomatoes, halved
- 1/4 cup black olives, sliced
- 1/4 cup parmesan cheese, grated
- Salt and pepper to taste

Instructions:

1. **Cook Pasta:** Cook pasta according to package instructions. Drain and cool slightly.
2. **Combine Ingredients:** In a large bowl, mix pasta, pesto, sun-dried tomatoes, cherry tomatoes, olives, and parmesan cheese.
3. **Season:** Add salt and pepper to taste, and toss to combine. Serve chilled or at room temperature.

Cabbage and Apple Salad with Pecans

Ingredients:

- 4 cups green cabbage, shredded
- 1 apple, cored and thinly sliced (Granny Smith or Fuji)
- 1/2 cup pecans, toasted
- 1/4 cup dried cranberries
- 1/4 cup red onion, thinly sliced

For the Dressing:

- 3 tablespoons apple cider vinegar
- 2 tablespoons olive oil
- 1 tablespoon honey
- Salt and pepper to taste

Instructions:

1. **Combine Salad Ingredients:** In a large bowl, toss cabbage, apple, pecans, cranberries, and red onion.
2. **Make Dressing:** In a small bowl, whisk together apple cider vinegar, olive oil, honey, salt, and pepper.
3. **Dress the Salad:** Drizzle dressing over the salad, toss to combine, and serve immediately.

Thai Mango Salad with Lime Dressing

Ingredients:

- 2 ripe mangoes, julienned
- 2 cups shredded carrots
- 1 red bell pepper, julienned
- 1/4 cup fresh cilantro, chopped
- 1/4 cup green onions, sliced
- 1/4 cup peanuts, chopped

For the Dressing:

- 3 tablespoons lime juice
- 2 tablespoons fish sauce
- 1 tablespoon sugar
- 1 clove garlic, minced

Instructions:

1. **Combine Salad Ingredients:** In a large bowl, combine mangoes, carrots, bell pepper, cilantro, and green onions.
2. **Make Dressing:** In a small bowl, whisk together lime juice, fish sauce, sugar, and garlic.
3. **Dress the Salad:** Pour dressing over the salad, toss gently, and top with chopped peanuts before serving.

Couscous Salad with Chickpeas and Veggies

Ingredients:

- 1 cup couscous
- 1 1/4 cups vegetable broth or water
- 1 can (15 oz) chickpeas, rinsed and drained
- 1 cucumber, diced
- 1 bell pepper, diced
- 1/2 cup cherry tomatoes, halved
- 1/4 cup parsley, chopped
- Salt and pepper to taste

For the Dressing:

- 3 tablespoons olive oil
- 2 tablespoons lemon juice
- 1 teaspoon cumin

Instructions:

1. **Cook Couscous:** Bring vegetable broth or water to a boil. Stir in couscous, remove from heat, cover, and let sit for 5 minutes. Fluff with a fork.
2. **Combine Ingredients:** In a large bowl, mix couscous, chickpeas, cucumber, bell pepper, cherry tomatoes, and parsley.
3. **Make Dressing:** In a small bowl, whisk together olive oil, lemon juice, cumin, salt, and pepper.
4. **Dress the Salad:** Drizzle dressing over the salad, toss to combine, and serve chilled.

Grilled Chicken Salad with Avocado

Ingredients:

- 2 grilled chicken breasts, sliced
- 4 cups mixed greens
- 1 avocado, sliced
- 1/2 cup cherry tomatoes, halved
- 1/4 red onion, thinly sliced
- 1/4 cup feta cheese, crumbled

For the Dressing:

- 3 tablespoons olive oil
- 1 tablespoon balsamic vinegar
- Salt and pepper to taste

Instructions:

1. **Combine Salad Ingredients:** In a large bowl, toss mixed greens, avocado, cherry tomatoes, red onion, and feta cheese.
2. **Add Chicken:** Top the salad with sliced grilled chicken.
3. **Make Dressing:** In a small bowl, whisk together olive oil, balsamic vinegar, salt, and pepper.
4. **Dress the Salad:** Drizzle dressing over the salad and serve immediately.

Roasted Cauliflower Salad with Tahini

Ingredients:

- 1 head cauliflower, cut into florets
- 2 tablespoons olive oil
- 1 teaspoon cumin
- Salt and pepper to taste
- 4 cups mixed greens
- 1/4 cup tahini
- 2 tablespoons lemon juice
- 1/4 cup fresh parsley, chopped

Instructions:

1. **Roast Cauliflower:** Preheat oven to 425°F (220°C). Toss cauliflower with olive oil, cumin, salt, and pepper. Roast for 25-30 minutes until golden.
2. **Combine Salad Ingredients:** In a large bowl, combine mixed greens and roasted cauliflower.
3. **Make Tahini Dressing:** In a small bowl, whisk together tahini, lemon juice, and a bit of water until smooth. Adjust consistency with water as needed.
4. **Dress the Salad:** Drizzle tahini dressing over the salad, toss gently, and top with chopped parsley before serving.

Mixed Bean Salad with Italian Dressing

Ingredients:

- 1 can (15 oz) kidney beans, rinsed and drained
- 1 can (15 oz) black beans, rinsed and drained
- 1 can (15 oz) chickpeas, rinsed and drained
- 1 cup cherry tomatoes, halved
- 1/4 cup red onion, diced
- 1/4 cup fresh parsley, chopped

For the Dressing:

- 1/4 cup olive oil
- 2 tablespoons red wine vinegar
- 1 teaspoon Italian seasoning
- Salt and pepper to taste

Instructions:

1. **Combine Salad Ingredients:** In a large bowl, mix kidney beans, black beans, chickpeas, cherry tomatoes, red onion, and parsley.
2. **Make Dressing:** In a small bowl, whisk together olive oil, red wine vinegar, Italian seasoning, salt, and pepper.
3. **Dress the Salad:** Pour dressing over the salad, toss to combine, and serve immediately or refrigerate for an hour for flavors to meld.

Strawberry Spinach Salad with Almonds

Ingredients:

- 4 cups fresh spinach leaves
- 1 cup strawberries, sliced
- 1/4 cup sliced almonds, toasted
- 1/4 cup feta cheese, crumbled
- 1/4 red onion, thinly sliced

For the Dressing:

- 3 tablespoons olive oil
- 2 tablespoons balsamic vinegar
- 1 tablespoon honey
- Salt and pepper to taste

Instructions:

1. **Combine Salad Ingredients:** In a large bowl, toss spinach, strawberries, almonds, feta cheese, and red onion.
2. **Make Dressing:** In a small bowl, whisk together olive oil, balsamic vinegar, honey, salt, and pepper.
3. **Dress the Salad:** Drizzle dressing over the salad just before serving and toss gently.

Grilled Chicken Caesar Salad

Ingredients:

- 2 grilled chicken breasts, sliced
- 4 cups romaine lettuce, chopped
- 1/2 cup croutons
- 1/4 cup parmesan cheese, grated

For the Dressing:

- 1/4 cup mayonnaise
- 2 tablespoons lemon juice
- 1 tablespoon Dijon mustard
- 1 teaspoon Worcestershire sauce
- Salt and pepper to taste

Instructions:

1. **Combine Salad Ingredients:** In a large bowl, combine romaine lettuce, grilled chicken, croutons, and parmesan cheese.
2. **Make Dressing:** In a small bowl, whisk together mayonnaise, lemon juice, Dijon mustard, Worcestershire sauce, salt, and pepper.
3. **Dress the Salad:** Pour dressing over the salad, toss to combine, and serve immediately.

Rainbow Salad with Bell Peppers and Carrots

Ingredients:

- 2 cups mixed greens
- 1 red bell pepper, sliced
- 1 yellow bell pepper, sliced
- 1 cup shredded carrots
- 1/2 cup cucumber, sliced
- 1/4 cup red onion, thinly sliced

For the Dressing:

- 3 tablespoons olive oil
- 2 tablespoons apple cider vinegar
- 1 teaspoon honey
- Salt and pepper to taste

Instructions:

1. **Combine Salad Ingredients:** In a large bowl, toss mixed greens, bell peppers, carrots, cucumber, and red onion.
2. **Make Dressing:** In a small bowl, whisk together olive oil, apple cider vinegar, honey, salt, and pepper.
3. **Dress the Salad:** Drizzle dressing over the salad just before serving and toss gently.

Egg and Potato Salad with Mustard Dressing

Ingredients:

- 4 cups potatoes, boiled and diced
- 4 hard-boiled eggs, chopped
- 1/4 cup celery, diced
- 1/4 cup red onion, diced
- 1/4 cup pickles, diced

For the Dressing:

- 1/4 cup mayonnaise
- 2 tablespoons Dijon mustard
- 1 tablespoon apple cider vinegar
- Salt and pepper to taste

Instructions:

1. **Combine Salad Ingredients:** In a large bowl, mix potatoes, eggs, celery, red onion, and pickles.
2. **Make Dressing:** In a small bowl, whisk together mayonnaise, Dijon mustard, apple cider vinegar, salt, and pepper.
3. **Dress the Salad:** Pour dressing over the salad, toss to combine, and serve chilled.

Lobster Salad with Lemon and Dill

Ingredients:

- 2 cups cooked lobster meat, chopped
- 4 cups mixed greens
- 1/4 cup cherry tomatoes, halved
- 1/4 cup cucumber, diced
- 1/4 cup red onion, thinly sliced

For the Dressing:

- 1/4 cup mayonnaise
- 2 tablespoons lemon juice
- 1 tablespoon fresh dill, chopped
- Salt and pepper to taste

Instructions:

1. **Combine Salad Ingredients:** In a large bowl, mix lobster meat, mixed greens, cherry tomatoes, cucumber, and red onion.
2. **Make Dressing:** In a small bowl, whisk together mayonnaise, lemon juice, dill, salt, and pepper.
3. **Dress the Salad:** Drizzle dressing over the salad and toss gently before serving.

Green Bean Salad with Cherry Tomatoes

Ingredients:

- 2 cups green beans, trimmed and blanched
- 1 cup cherry tomatoes, halved
- 1/4 cup red onion, thinly sliced
- 1/4 cup feta cheese, crumbled
- 1/4 cup walnuts, chopped

For the Dressing:

- 3 tablespoons olive oil
- 2 tablespoons red wine vinegar
- 1 teaspoon Dijon mustard
- Salt and pepper to taste

Instructions:

1. **Combine Salad Ingredients:** In a large bowl, combine green beans, cherry tomatoes, red onion, feta cheese, and walnuts.
2. **Make Dressing:** In a small bowl, whisk together olive oil, red wine vinegar, Dijon mustard, salt, and pepper.
3. **Dress the Salad:** Drizzle dressing over the salad and toss to combine before serving.

Asian Cabbage Salad with Sesame Dressing

Ingredients:

- 4 cups green cabbage, shredded
- 1 cup carrots, grated
- 1 red bell pepper, sliced
- 1/4 cup green onions, sliced
- 1/4 cup cilantro, chopped
- 1/4 cup sesame seeds, toasted

For the Dressing:

- 1/4 cup soy sauce
- 2 tablespoons rice vinegar
- 2 tablespoons sesame oil
- 1 tablespoon honey
- 1 teaspoon grated ginger

Instructions:

1. **Combine Salad Ingredients:** In a large bowl, mix cabbage, carrots, bell pepper, green onions, cilantro, and sesame seeds.
2. **Make Dressing:** In a small bowl, whisk together soy sauce, rice vinegar, sesame oil, honey, and ginger.
3. **Dress the Salad:** Pour dressing over the salad, toss to combine, and serve immediately.

Mediterranean Chickpea Salad

Ingredients:

- 1 can (15 oz) chickpeas, rinsed and drained
- 1 cucumber, diced
- 1 cup cherry tomatoes, halved
- 1/4 cup red onion, diced
- 1/4 cup kalamata olives, pitted and sliced
- 1/4 cup feta cheese, crumbled
- 1/4 cup parsley, chopped

For the Dressing:

- 3 tablespoons olive oil
- 2 tablespoons lemon juice
- 1 teaspoon dried oregano
- Salt and pepper to taste

Instructions:

1. **Combine Salad Ingredients:** In a large bowl, mix chickpeas, cucumber, cherry tomatoes, red onion, olives, feta cheese, and parsley.
2. **Make Dressing:** In a small bowl, whisk together olive oil, lemon juice, oregano, salt, and pepper.
3. **Dress the Salad:** Drizzle dressing over the salad, toss to combine, and serve immediately or chill for a bit before serving.

Antipasto Salad with Salami and Cheese

Ingredients:

- 4 cups mixed greens
- 1 cup salami, sliced
- 1 cup mozzarella cheese, cubed
- 1/2 cup cherry tomatoes, halved
- 1/4 cup black olives, sliced
- 1/4 cup roasted red peppers, sliced
- 1/4 cup red onion, thinly sliced

For the Dressing:

- 3 tablespoons olive oil
- 2 tablespoons red wine vinegar
- 1 teaspoon Italian seasoning
- Salt and pepper to taste

Instructions:

1. **Combine Salad Ingredients:** In a large bowl, toss together mixed greens, salami, mozzarella, cherry tomatoes, olives, roasted red peppers, and red onion.
2. **Make Dressing:** In a small bowl, whisk together olive oil, red wine vinegar, Italian seasoning, salt, and pepper.
3. **Dress the Salad:** Drizzle dressing over the salad just before serving and toss gently.

Smoked Salmon Salad with Capers

Ingredients:

- 4 cups mixed greens
- 8 oz smoked salmon, sliced
- 1/4 cup red onion, thinly sliced
- 1/4 cup capers, drained
- 1/2 avocado, sliced
- 1/4 cup cream cheese, crumbled

For the Dressing:

- 2 tablespoons olive oil
- 1 tablespoon lemon juice
- Salt and pepper to taste

Instructions:

1. **Combine Salad Ingredients:** In a large bowl, mix together mixed greens, smoked salmon, red onion, capers, avocado, and cream cheese.
2. **Make Dressing:** In a small bowl, whisk together olive oil, lemon juice, salt, and pepper.
3. **Dress the Salad:** Drizzle dressing over the salad and toss gently before serving.

Kale Salad with Cranberries and Pecans

Ingredients:

- 4 cups kale, chopped
- 1/2 cup dried cranberries
- 1/2 cup pecans, toasted
- 1/4 cup feta cheese, crumbled
- 1/4 red onion, thinly sliced

For the Dressing:

- 3 tablespoons olive oil
- 1 tablespoon apple cider vinegar
- 1 tablespoon honey
- Salt and pepper to taste

Instructions:

1. **Combine Salad Ingredients:** In a large bowl, toss kale, cranberries, pecans, feta cheese, and red onion.
2. **Make Dressing:** In a small bowl, whisk together olive oil, apple cider vinegar, honey, salt, and pepper.
3. **Dress the Salad:** Drizzle dressing over the salad just before serving and toss gently.

Avocado and Black Bean Salad

Ingredients:

- 1 can (15 oz) black beans, rinsed and drained
- 1 avocado, diced
- 1 cup cherry tomatoes, halved
- 1/4 cup red onion, diced
- 1/4 cup cilantro, chopped
- 1 lime, juiced

For the Dressing:

- 3 tablespoons olive oil
- 1 teaspoon cumin
- Salt and pepper to taste

Instructions:

1. **Combine Salad Ingredients:** In a large bowl, mix black beans, avocado, cherry tomatoes, red onion, cilantro, and lime juice.
2. **Make Dressing:** In a small bowl, whisk together olive oil, cumin, salt, and pepper.
3. **Dress the Salad:** Drizzle dressing over the salad and toss gently before serving.

Roasted Tomato Salad with Fresh Basil

Ingredients:

- 2 cups cherry tomatoes, halved
- 2 tablespoons olive oil
- Salt and pepper to taste
- 1/4 cup fresh basil leaves, torn
- 1/4 cup balsamic vinegar
- 1/4 cup feta cheese, crumbled (optional)

Instructions:

1. **Roast the Tomatoes:** Preheat the oven to 400°F (200°C). Toss cherry tomatoes with olive oil, salt, and pepper on a baking sheet. Roast for 20-25 minutes until soft and caramelized.
2. **Combine Salad Ingredients:** In a large bowl, combine roasted tomatoes, fresh basil, and feta cheese if using.
3. **Dress the Salad:** Drizzle balsamic vinegar over the salad and toss gently before serving.

Chicken and Avocado Salad

Ingredients:

- 2 cups cooked chicken breast, shredded
- 1 avocado, diced
- 1/2 cup cherry tomatoes, halved
- 1/4 cup red onion, diced
- 1/4 cup cilantro, chopped

For the Dressing:

- 3 tablespoons olive oil
- 1 tablespoon lime juice
- Salt and pepper to taste

Instructions:

1. **Combine Salad Ingredients:** In a large bowl, mix chicken, avocado, cherry tomatoes, red onion, and cilantro.
2. **Make Dressing:** In a small bowl, whisk together olive oil, lime juice, salt, and pepper.
3. **Dress the Salad:** Drizzle dressing over the salad and toss gently before serving.

Summer Fruit Salad with Honey Lime Dressing

Ingredients:

- 2 cups strawberries, hulled and sliced
- 2 cups watermelon, diced
- 2 cups cantaloupe, diced
- 1 cup blueberries
- 1/2 cup mint leaves, chopped

For the Dressing:

- 3 tablespoons honey
- 2 tablespoons lime juice

Instructions:

1. **Combine Fruit Ingredients:** In a large bowl, mix strawberries, watermelon, cantaloupe, blueberries, and mint leaves.
2. **Make Dressing:** In a small bowl, whisk together honey and lime juice until combined.
3. **Dress the Salad:** Drizzle honey lime dressing over the fruit salad just before serving and toss gently.

Tomato and Cucumber Salad with Dill

Ingredients:

- 2 cups tomatoes, diced
- 1 cucumber, diced
- 1/4 red onion, thinly sliced
- 1/4 cup fresh dill, chopped
- 1/4 cup feta cheese, crumbled (optional)

For the Dressing:

- 3 tablespoons olive oil
- 2 tablespoons red wine vinegar
- Salt and pepper to taste

Instructions:

1. **Combine Salad Ingredients:** In a large bowl, mix tomatoes, cucumber, red onion, dill, and feta cheese if using.
2. **Make Dressing:** In a small bowl, whisk together olive oil, red wine vinegar, salt, and pepper.
3. **Dress the Salad:** Drizzle dressing over the salad just before serving and toss gently.

Greek Orzo Salad with Lemon Dressing

Ingredients:

- 1 cup orzo pasta, cooked and cooled
- 1 cup cherry tomatoes, halved
- 1/2 cup cucumber, diced
- 1/4 cup red onion, diced
- 1/2 cup kalamata olives, pitted and sliced
- 1/4 cup feta cheese, crumbled
- 1/4 cup parsley, chopped

For the Dressing:

- 3 tablespoons olive oil
- 2 tablespoons lemon juice
- 1 teaspoon dried oregano
- Salt and pepper to taste

Instructions:

1. **Combine Salad Ingredients:** In a large bowl, combine cooked orzo, cherry tomatoes, cucumber, red onion, olives, feta cheese, and parsley.
2. **Make Dressing:** In a small bowl, whisk together olive oil, lemon juice, oregano, salt, and pepper.
3. **Dress the Salad:** Drizzle dressing over the salad, toss to combine, and serve immediately or chill before serving.

www.ingramcontent.com/pod-product-compliance
Lightning Source LLC
LaVergne TN
LVHW081504060526
838201LV00056BA/2928